3

american popular piano

TECHNIC

Created by
Dr. Scott McBride Smith

Series Composer
Christopher Norton

Editor
Dr. Scott McBride Smith

Associate Editor
Clarke MacIntosh

Book Design & Engraving
Andrew Jones

Cover Design
Wagner Design

Introduction

Although many books concerned with developing pianistic skills use the word "technique", we prefer to think in terms of "technic". That's because the root word for technic is the ancient Greek tekhnikos – "about art". Think about it. How can you play the piano beautifully without art? And how can you express yourself if you can't control your fingers?

The famous playwright Oscar Wilde said that technic is just another name for personality. He's right. If you don't have a good technic, you will never be able to express your own individuality in your playing. Your ideas may be fresh, your feeling sincere – but if you can't control your fingers, your playing will be lacking.

The theory behind *American Popular Piano Technic* books is simple: provide students with the physical tools for personal expression. Early volumes concentrate primarily on finger technic. But don't forget that you play the piano with your whole body. The fundamentals of good technic are consistent for all levels.

Make sure that:

- your posture is good and that you are sitting correctly.

- your shoulders are down and your arms relaxed.

- your arm is aligned directly behind the note that is playing. Some sideways arm motion will be necessary to achieve this. Many teachers call this "rotation".

- you relax your finger at the bottom of the key. It's not necessary to continue pressing once the note has sounded.

- you repeat each drill many times, listening closely and with concentration. Make sure that it sounds good and feels right.

You may want to proceed through all the exercises in C Major before adding new keys. This is a good idea for some students since the exercises do get a bit harder as they progress. You may want to do each exercise in all keys before moving on. This works too, as long as you don't get bogged down on any one exercise. Which approach works for you? Try both and see.

Does it sound easy? It is – but it takes a lifetime of work to achieve true control and simplicity! Every athlete spends time on drills, exercises and warm-ups outside of the game. Pianists, too, should spend time working on their technic outside of the repertoire pieces. When your piano fundamentals become strong, you will learn more easily and perform more confidently.

Do you want to express yourself in your piano playing? *American Popular Piano Technic* books will help. But they won't work if you don't! Practice carefully and often. Spend time developing your skills – and your skills will help you develop your own personal expression.

Library and Archives Canada Cataloguing in Publication

Smith, Scott McBride

American popular piano [music] : technic / created by Scott McBride Smith ;
series composer, Christopher Norton ;
editor, Scott McBride Smith ; associate editor, Clarke MacIntosh.

To be complete in 11 volumes.
Publisher's nos.: APP T-00 (level P); APP T-01 (level 1); APP T-02 (level 2).
Contents: Preparatory level -- Level 1 -- Level 2.
Miscellaneous information: The series is organized in 11 levels, from preparatory to level 10, each including a repertoire album, an etudes album, a skills book, a "technic" book, and an instrumental backings compact disc.

ISBN 978-1-897379-33-2 (preparatory level).--ISBN 978-1-897379-34-9 (level 1).--ISBN 978-1-897379-35-6 (level 2).--
ISBN 978-1-897379-36-3 (level 3).--ISBN 978-1-897379-37-0 (level 4).--ISBN 978-1-897379-38-7 (level 5)

1. Musical intervals and scales. 2. Piano--Studies and exercises. 3. Musical intervals and scales--Juvenile literature.
4. Piano--Studies and exercises--Juvenile. I. Norton, Christopher, 1953- II. MacIntosh, S. Clarke, 1959- III. Title.

LEVEL 3 TECHNIC
Table of Contents

Introduction ii

Scales & Triads

C Major
Scales 2
Triads 4

G Major
Scales 6
Triads 8

D Major
Scales 10
Triads 12

c harmonic minor
Scales 14
Triads 16

g harmonic minor
Scales 18
Triads 20

A Major
Scales 22
Triads 24

E Major
Scales 26
Triads 28

d harmonic minor
Scales 30
Triads 32

Arpeggios

C Major 34
G Major 36
F Major 38
a minor 40
e minor 42
d minor 44

Drills

C Major 46
G Major 48
c harmonic minor 50
g harmonic minor 52
D Major 54
A Major 56
d harmonic minor 58
a harmonic minor 60

How to Use this Book 62

Technic Tracker .... inside back cover

Scales: C Major

Basic Patterns

No. 1

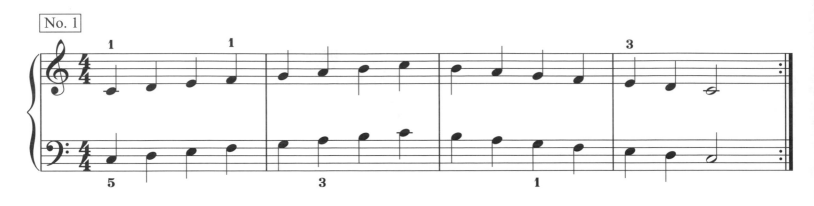

No. 2

No. 3

No. 4

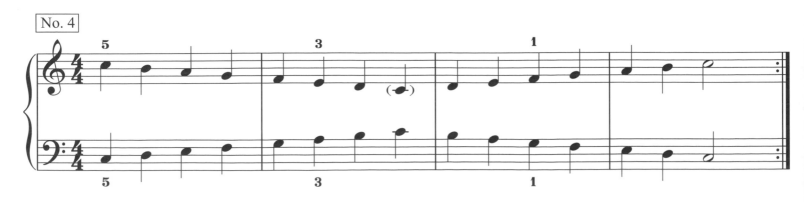

Complementary Patterns

No. 5

No. 6

No. 7

No. 8

Triads: C Major

Cadences

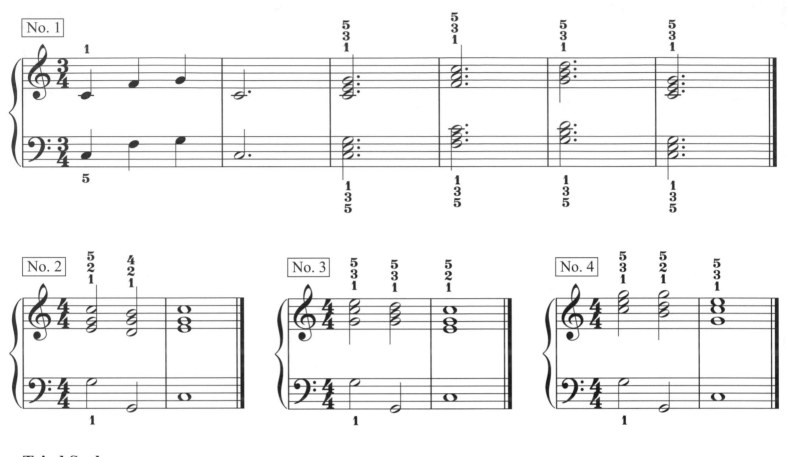

Triad Scales

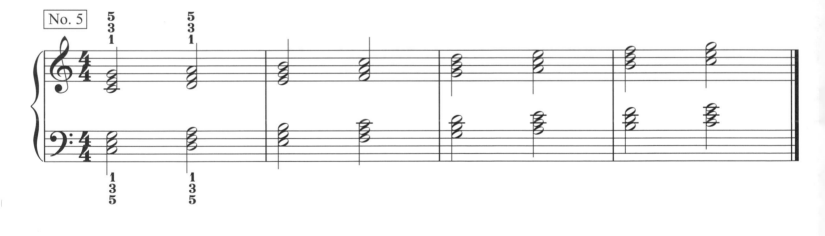

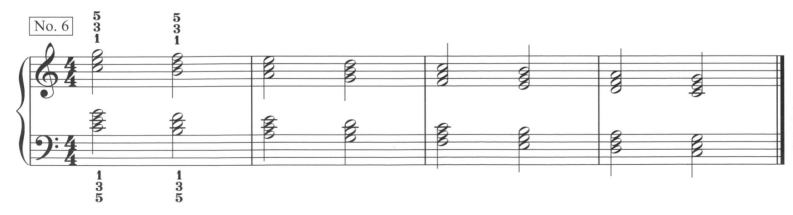

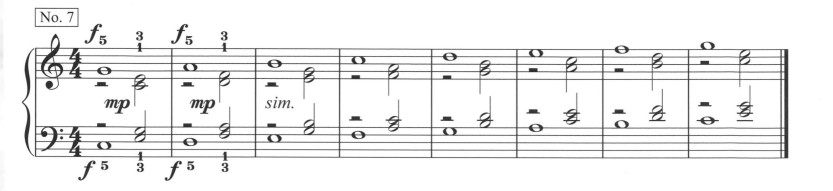

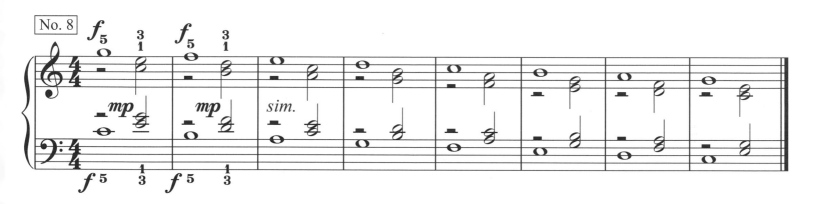

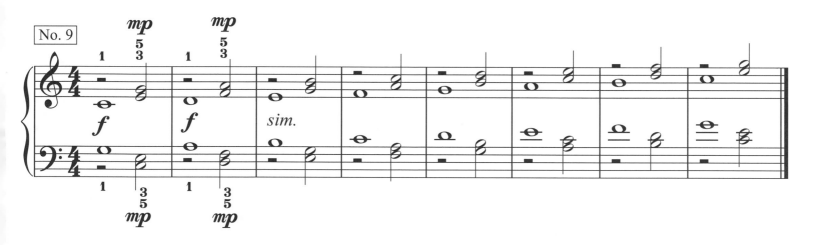

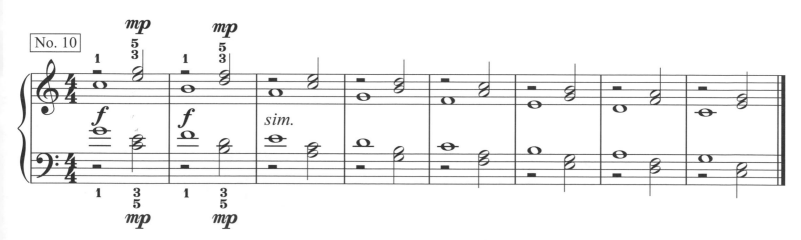

Scales: G Major

Basic Patterns

No. 1

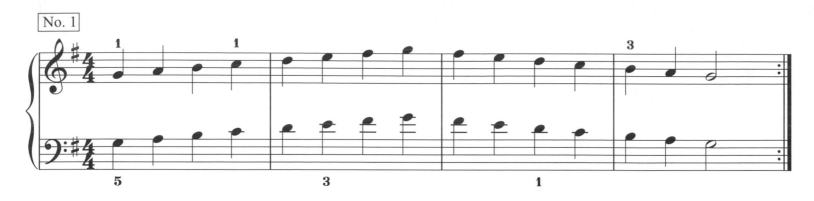

No. 2

No. 3

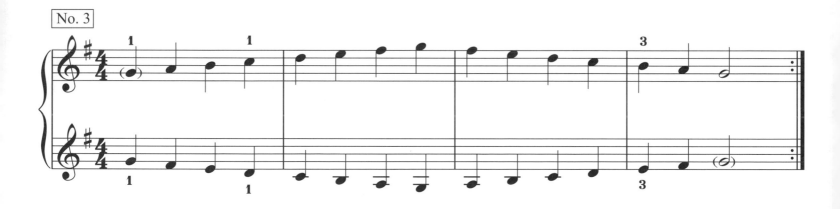

No. 4

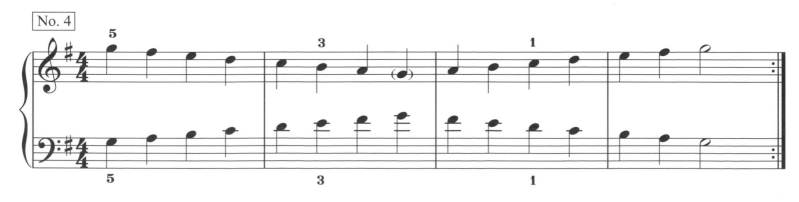

Complementary Patterns

No. 5

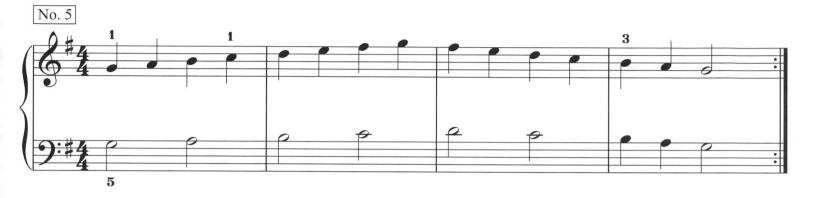

No. 6

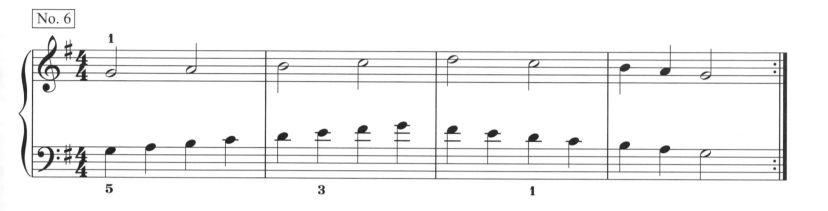

No. 7

No. 8

Triads: G Major

Cadences

Triad Scales

Scales: D Major

Basic Patterns

No. 1

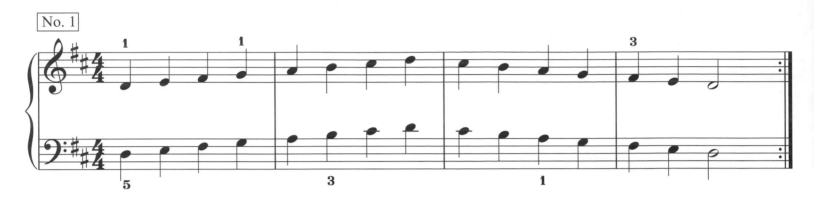

No. 2

No. 3

No. 4

Complementary Patterns

No. 5

No. 6

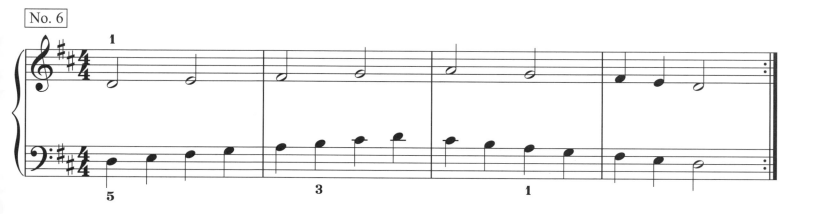

No. 7

No. 8

Triads: D Major

Cadences

Triad Scales

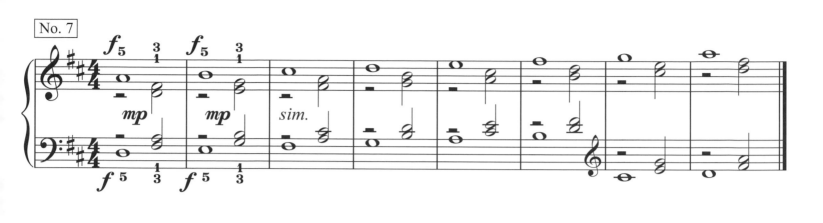

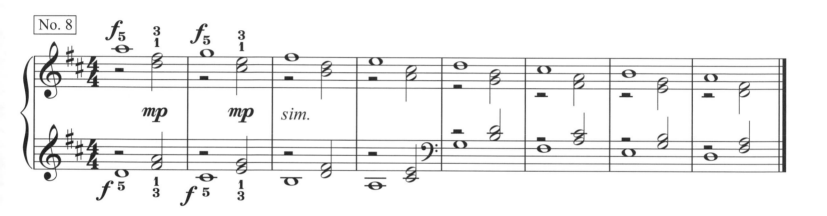

Scales: c harmonic minor

Basic Patterns

No. 1

No. 2

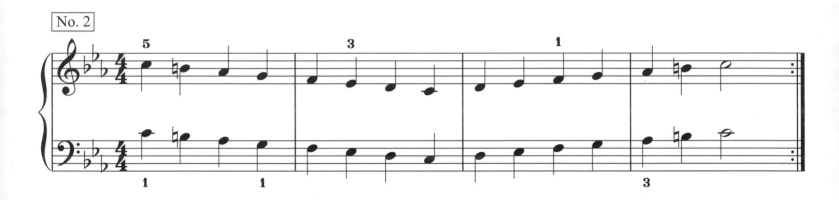

No. 3

No. 4

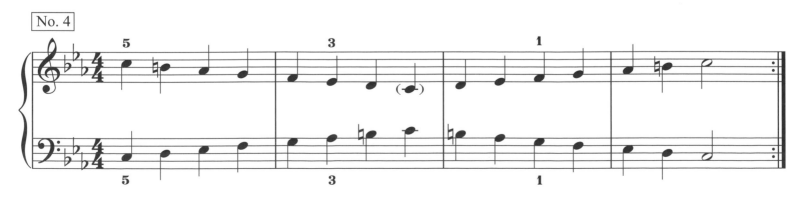

Complementary Patterns

No. 5

No. 6

No. 7

No. 8

Triads: c harmonic minor

Cadences

Triad Scales

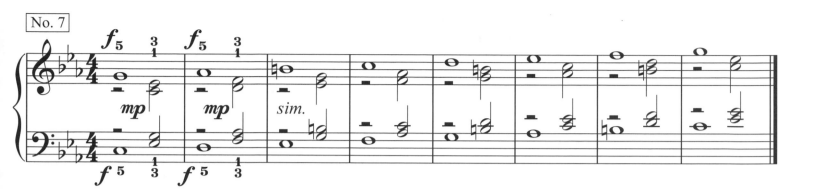

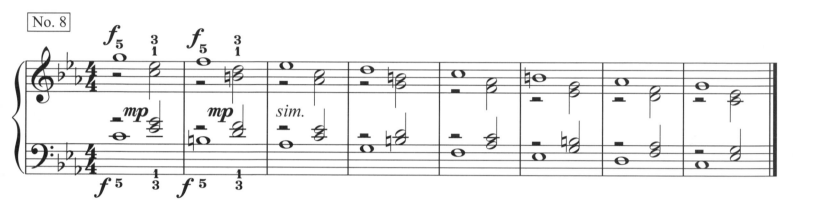

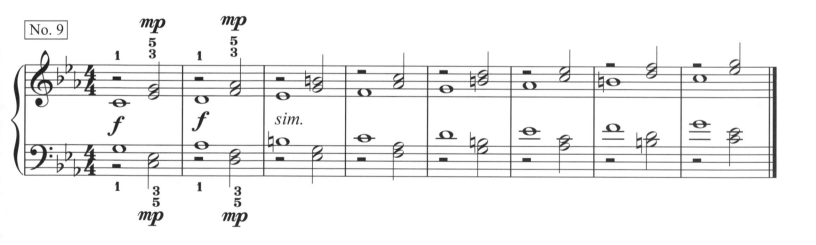

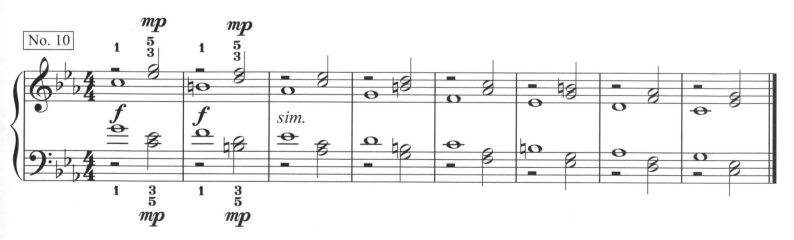

Scales: g harmonic minor

Basic Patterns

No. 1

No. 2

No. 3

No. 4

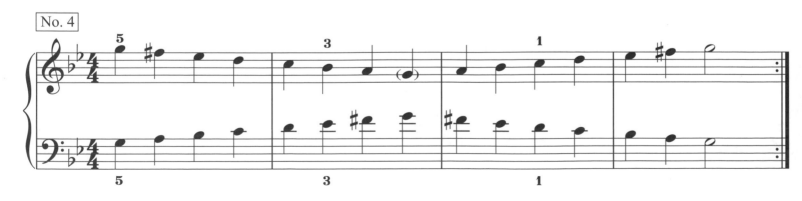

Complementary Patterns

No. 5

No. 6

No. 7

No. 8

20

Triads: g harmonic minor

Cadences

Triad Scales

Scales: A Major

Basic Patterns

No. 1

No. 2
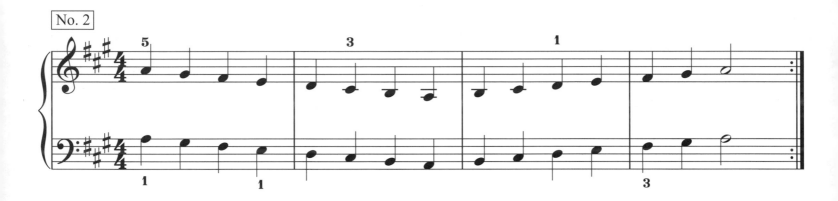

No. 3

No. 4

Complementary Patterns

No. 5

No. 6

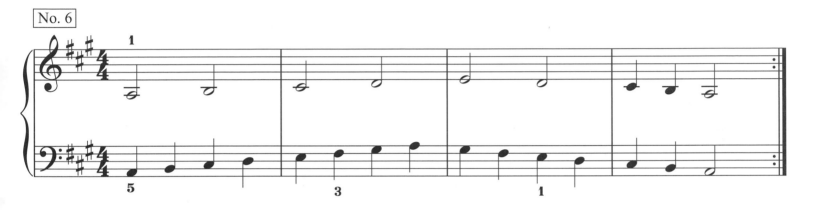

No. 7

No. 8

Triads: A Major

Cadences

Triad Scales

No. 7

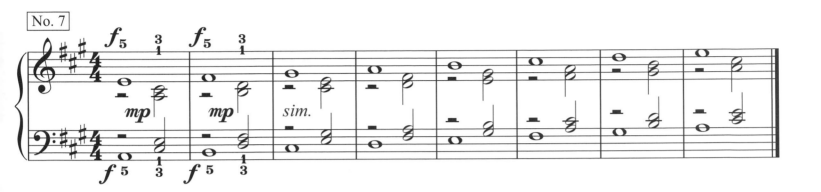

No. 8

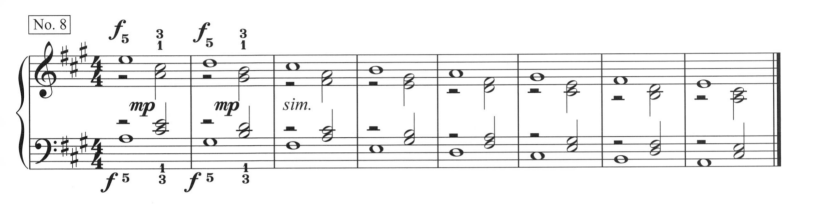

No. 9

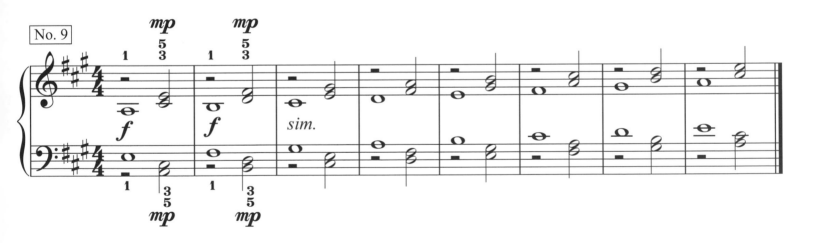

No. 10

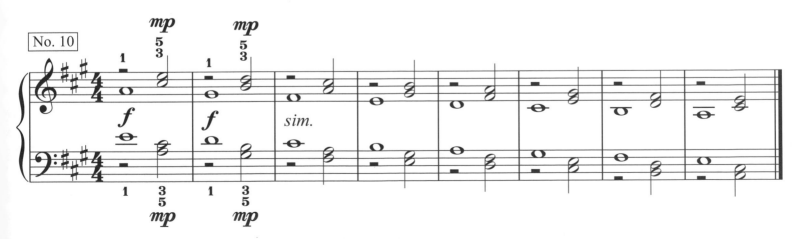

Scales: E Major

Basic Patterns

No. 1

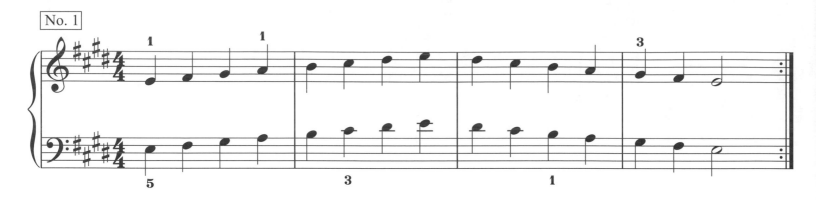

No. 2

No. 3

No. 4

Complementary Patterns

No. 5

No. 6
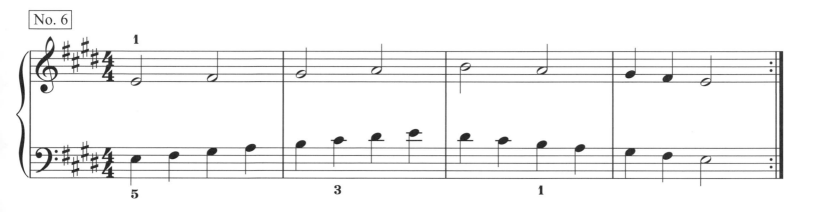

No. 7

No. 8

Triads: E Major

Cadences

Triad Scales

No. 7

No. 8

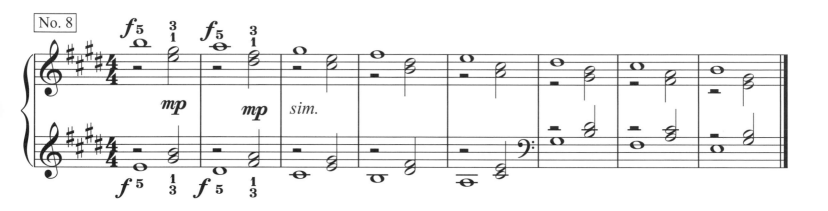

No. 9

No. 10

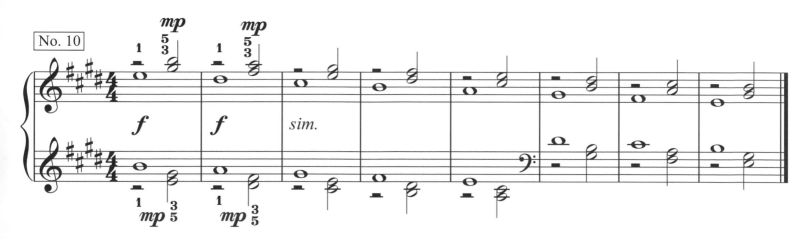

Scales: d harmonic minor

Basic Patterns

No. 1

No. 2

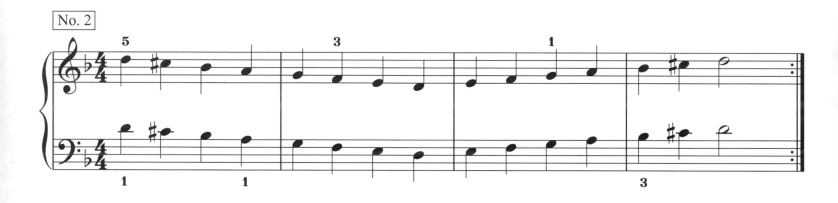

No. 3

No. 4

Complementary Patterns

No. 5

No. 6

No. 7

No. 8

Triads: d harmonic minor

Cadences

Triad Scales

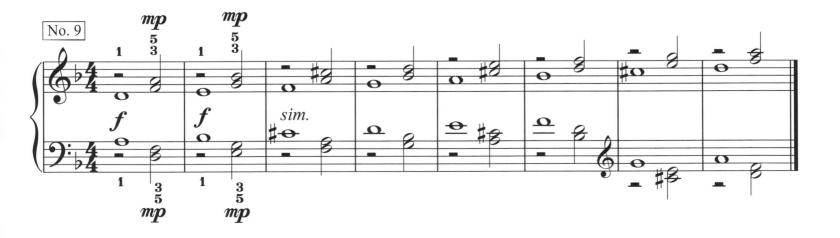

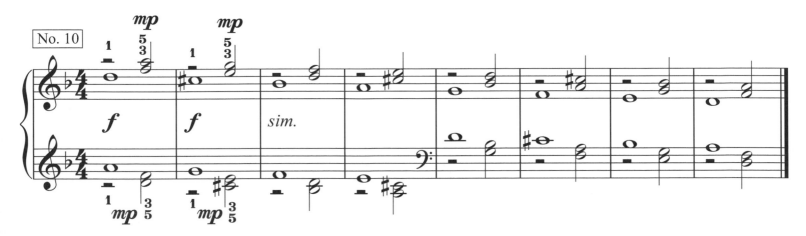

Arpeggios: C Major

No. 1

No. 2

No. 3

No. 4

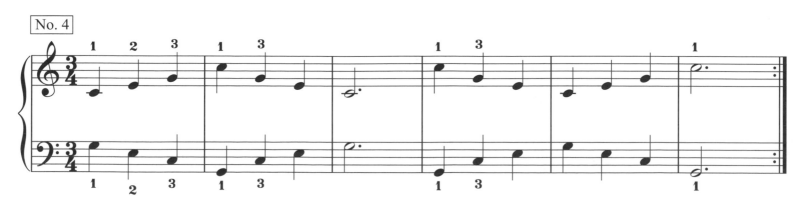

Arpeggios: G Major

No. 1

No. 2

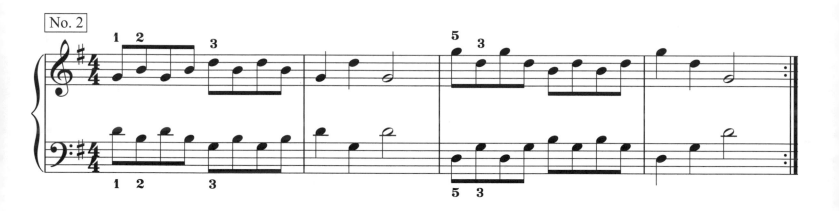

No. 3

No. 4

Arpeggios: F Major

No. 1

No. 2

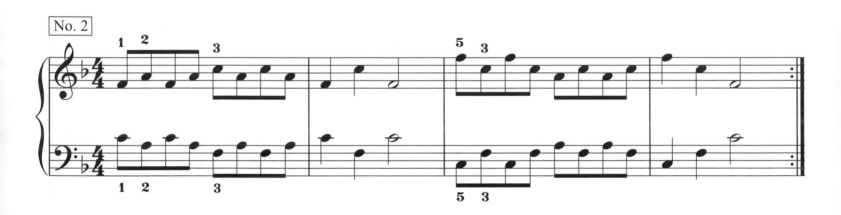

No. 3

No. 4

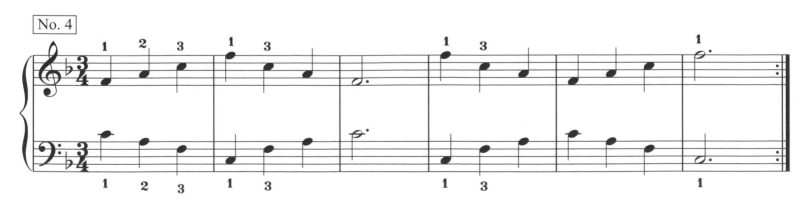

Arpeggios: a harmonic minor

No. 1

No. 2

No. 3

No. 4

Arpeggios: e harmonic minor

No. 1

No. 2

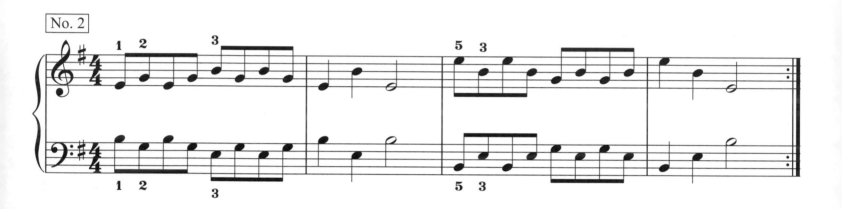

No. 3

No. 4

Arpeggios: d harmonic minor

No. 1

No. 2

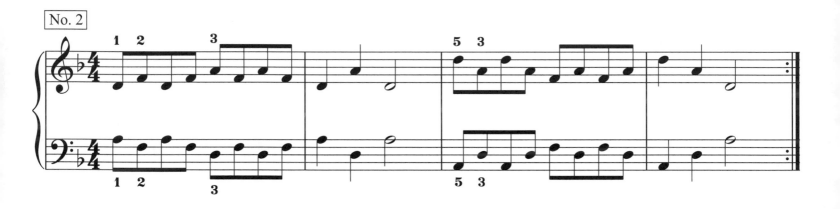

No. 3

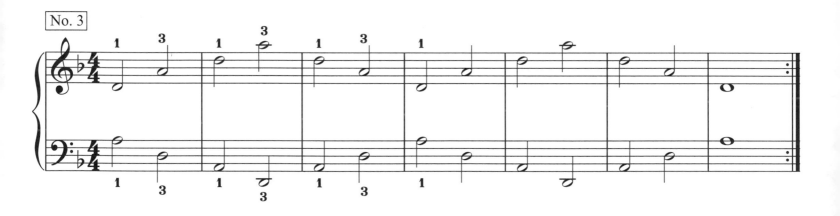

No. 4

45

Drills: C Major

Arm Weight Exercises

a) Rest one arm on top of your other arm.

b) Experiment with making the top arm heavy, then light. Do this by letting the arm relax down with its own weight, not by pushing.

c) Rest your third finger on the surface of the key. Play each note by gently "releasing" your arm weight into the key as you did in step b). Your wrist should not move below the level of the key.

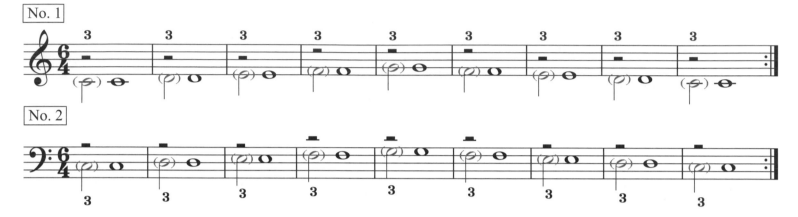

One-Note Drawbridge Exercises

a) Lift your arm about 6 inches above the key without bending at the wrist – as if it were a drawbridge. Flex your third finger so it feels strong.

b) Play each note by dropping your third finger into the key, releasing your arm weight with energy. Your wrist should not drop below key level.

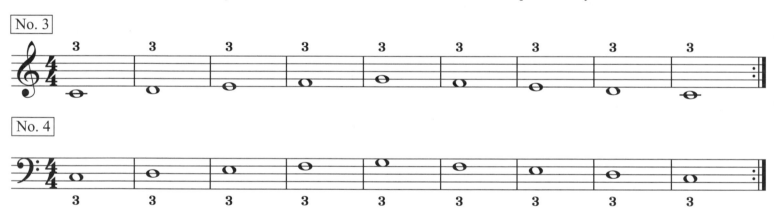

Open-Fifth Drawbridge Exercises

a) Lift your arm about 8 inches above the key without bending at the wrist – as if it were a drawbridge. Flex your thumb and fifth fingers so they feel strong.

b) Play each fifth by dropping your fingers into the keys, releasing your arm weight with energy. Your wrist should not drop below key level.

c) Repeat steps a) & b), but this time lift your arm about 4 inches above the keys.

d) Repeat steps a) & b) lifting only 1 inch above the keys.

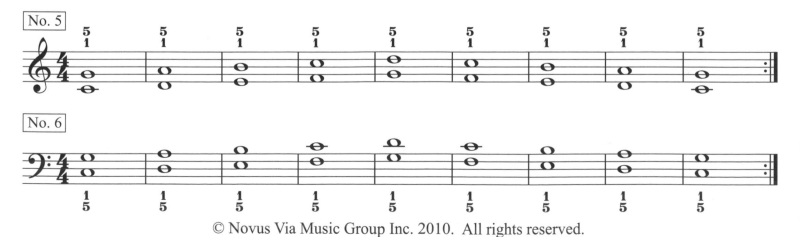

Beginning Rotation Exercises – Inward

a) Place your hand on the keys, fingers covering the five notes of the pentascale, with a good hand position.

b) Pretend you are getting ready to open a door. Rotate your hand inward, towards your thumb. The rotation motion should play the first note.

Observe that:

    i)   Your thumb will turn to be resting slightly on its nail.

    ii) Your elbow will move slightly away from your body.

    iii) The other fingers will raise above the keys.

c) Play the second note by rotating the other direction, back into position.

Beginning Rotation Exercises – Outward

a) Place your hand on the keys, fingers covering the five notes of the pentascale, with a good hand position.

b) Pretend you are getting ready to open a door. Rotate your hand outward, towards your 5th finger. The rotation motion should play the first note.

Observe that:

    i)   Your third finger will turn slightly onto its nail.

    ii) Your elbow will move slightly in to your body.

    iii) The thumb and second fingers will raise off the keys.

c) Play the second note by rotating the other direction, back into position.

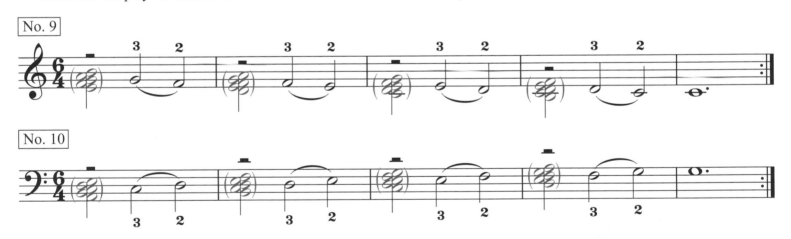

Fingering Variations

When you are able to play Drill nos. 7-10 with a fluid, even motion, move on to these variations which use different fingerings. Work through these before moving on to a new key.

Drills: G Major

Arm Weight Exercises

a) Rest one arm on top of your other arm.

b) Experiment with making the top arm heavy, then light. Do this by letting the arm relax down with its own weight, not by pushing.

c) Rest your third finger on the surface of the key. Play each note by gently "releasing" your arm weight into the key as you did in step b). Your wrist should not move below the level of the key.

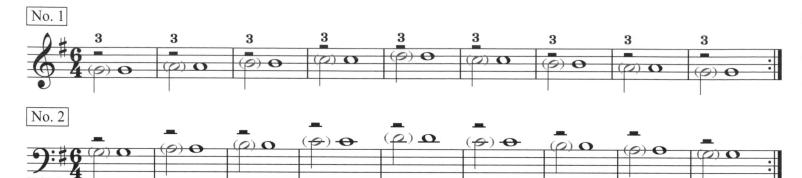

One-Note Drawbridge Exercises

a) Lift your arm about 6 inches above the key without bending at the wrist – as if it were a drawbridge. Flex your third finger so it feels strong.

b) Play each note by dropping your third finger into the key, releasing your arm weight with energy. Your wrist should not drop below key level.

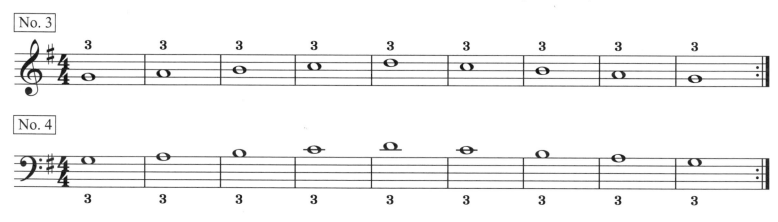

Open-Fifth Drawbridge Exercises

a) Lift your arm about 8 inches above the key without bending at the wrist – as if it were a drawbridge. Flex your thumb and fifth fingers so they feel strong.

b) Play each fifth by dropping your fingers into the keys,

releasing your arm weight with energy. Your wrist should not drop below key level.

c) Repeat steps a) & b), but this time lift your arm about 4 inches above the keys.

d) Repeat steps a) & b) lifting only 1 inch above the keys.

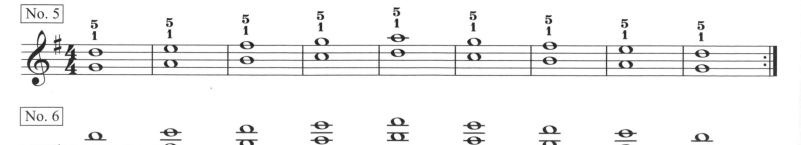

Beginning Rotation Exercises – Inward

a) Place your hand on the keys, fingers covering the five notes of the pentascale, with a good hand position.

b) Pretend you are getting ready to open a door. Rotate your hand inward, towards your thumb. The rotation motion should play the first note.

Observe that:

   i)   Your thumb will turn to be resting slightly on its nail.

   ii) Your elbow will move slightly away from your body.

  iii) The other fingers will raise above the keys.

c) Play the second note by rotating the other direction, back into position.

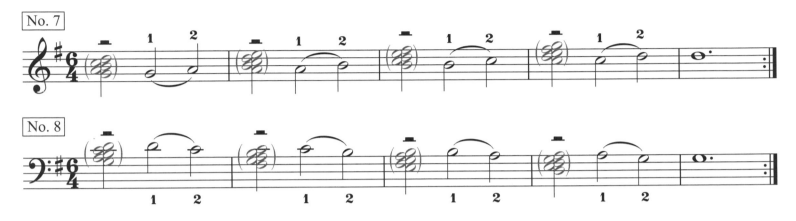

Beginning Rotation Exercises – Outward

a) Place your hand on the keys, fingers covering the five notes of the pentascale, with a good hand position.

b) Pretend you are getting ready to open a door. Rotate your hand outward, towards your 5th finger. The rotation motion should play the first note.

Observe that:

   i)   Your third finger will turn slightly onto its nail.

   ii) Your elbow will move slightly in to your body.

  iii) The thumb and second fingers will raise off the keys.

c) Play the second note by rotating the other direction, back into position.

Fingering Variations

When you are able to play Drill nos. 7-10 with a fluid, even motion, move on to these variations which use different fingerings. Work through these before moving on to a new key.

Drills: c harmonic minor

Arm Weight Exercises

a) Rest one arm on top of your other arm.
b) Experiment with making the top arm heavy, then light. Do this by letting the arm relax down with its own weight, not by pushing.

c) Rest your third finger on the surface of the key. Play each note by gently "releasing" your arm weight into the key as you did in step b). Your wrist should not move below the level of the key.

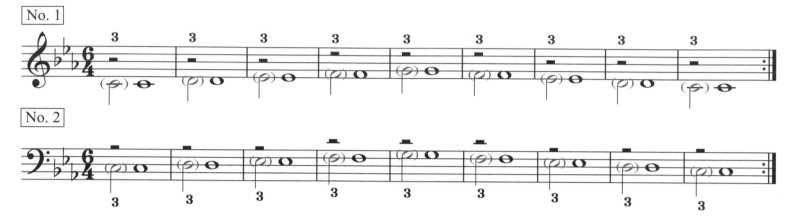

One-Note Drawbridge Exercises

a) Lift your arm about 6 inches above the key without bending at the wrist – as if it were a drawbridge. Flex your third finger so it feels strong.

b) Play each note by dropping your third finger into the key, releasing your arm weight with energy. Your wrist should not drop below key level.

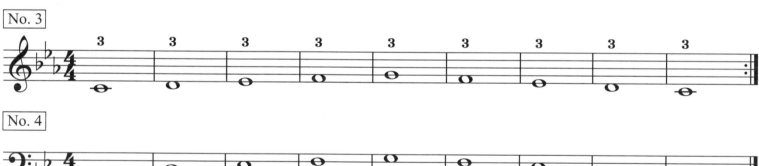

Open-Fifth Drawbridge Exercises

a) Lift your arm about 8 inches above the key without bending at the wrist – as if it were a drawbridge. Flex your thumb and fifth fingers so they feel strong.

b) Play each fifth by dropping your fingers into the keys,

releasing your arm weight with energy. Your wrist should not drop below key level.

c) Repeat steps a) & b), but this time lift your arm about 4 inches above the keys.

d) Repeat steps a) & b) lifting only 1 inch above the keys.

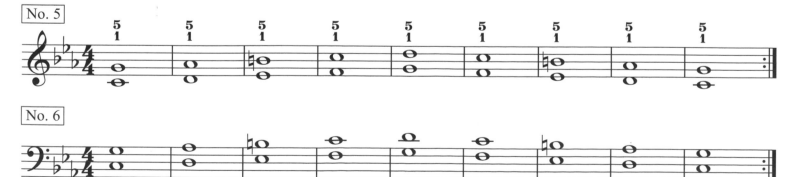

Beginning Rotation Exercises – Inward

a) Place your hand on the keys, fingers covering the five notes of the pentascale, with a good hand position.

b) Pretend you are getting ready to open a door. Rotate your hand inward, towards your thumb. The rotation motion should play the first note.

Observe that:

i) Your thumb will turn to be resting slightly on its nail.

ii) Your elbow will move slightly away from your body.

iii) The other fingers will raise above the keys.

c) Play the second note by rotating the other direction, back into position.

Beginning Rotation Exercises – Outward

a) Place your hand on the keys, fingers covering the five notes of the pentascale, with a good hand position.

b) Pretend you are getting ready to open a door. Rotate your hand outward, towards your 5th finger. The rotation motion should play the first note.

Observe that:

i) Your third finger will turn slightly onto its nail.

ii) Your elbow will move slightly in to your body.

iii) The thumb and second fingers will raise off the keys.

c) Play the second note by rotating the other direction, back into position.

Fingering Variations

When you are able to play Drill nos. 7-10 with a fluid, even motion, move on to these variations which use different fingerings. Work through these before moving on to a new key.

Drills: g harmonic minor

Arm Weight Exercises

a) Rest one arm on top of your other arm.

b) Experiment with making the top arm heavy, then light. Do this by letting the arm relax down with its own weight, not by pushing.

c) Rest your third finger on the surface of the key. Play each note by gently "releasing" your arm weight into the key as you did in step b). Your wrist should not move below the level of the key.

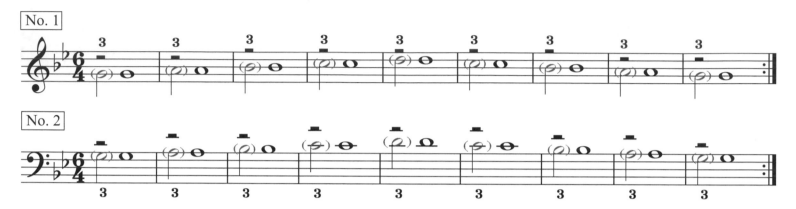

One-Note Drawbridge Exercises

a) Lift your arm about 6 inches above the key without bending at the wrist – as if it were a drawbridge. Flex your third finger so it feels strong.

b) Play each note by dropping your third finger into the key, releasing your arm weight with energy. Your wrist should not drop below key level.

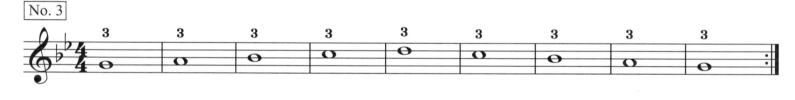

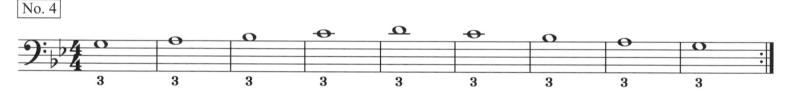

Open-Fifth Drawbridge Exercises

a) Lift your arm about 8 inches above the key without bending at the wrist – as if it were a drawbridge. Flex your thumb and fifth fingers so they feel strong.

b) Play each fifth by dropping your fingers into the keys,

releasing your arm weight with energy. Your wrist should not drop below key level.

c) Repeat steps a) & b), but this time lift your arm about 4 inches above the keys.

d) Repeat steps a) & b) lifting only 1 inch above the keys.

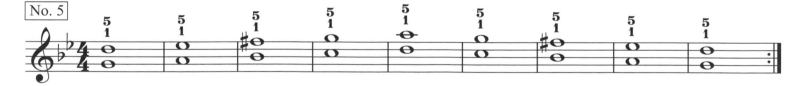

Beginning Rotation Exercises – Inward

a) Place your hand on the keys, fingers covering the five notes of the pentascale, with a good hand position.

b) Pretend you are getting ready to open a door. Rotate your hand inward, towards your thumb. The rotation motion should play the first note.

Observe that:
    i) Your thumb will turn to be resting slightly on its nail.
    ii) Your elbow will move slightly away from your body.
    iii) The other fingers will raise above the keys.

c) Play the second note by rotating the other direction, back into position.

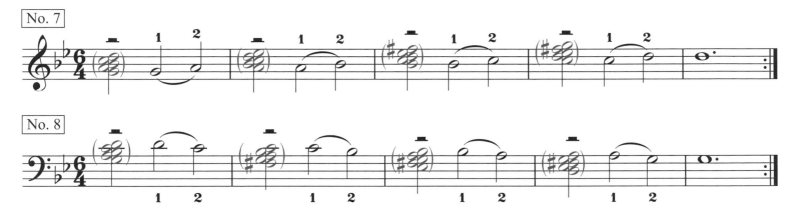

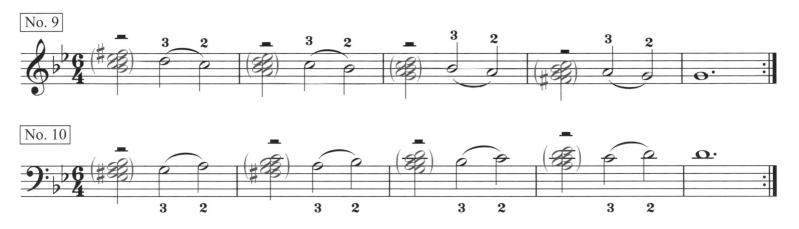

Beginning Rotation Exercises – Outward

a) Place your hand on the keys, fingers covering the five notes of the pentascale, with a good hand position.

b) Pretend you are getting ready to open a door. Rotate your hand outward, towards your 5th finger. The rotation motion should play the first note.

Observe that:
    i) Your third finger will turn slightly onto its nail.
    ii) Your elbow will move slightly in to your body.
    iii) The thumb and second fingers will raise off the keys.

c) Play the second note by rotating the other direction, back into position.

Fingering Variations

When you are able to play Drill nos. 7-10 with a fluid, even motion, move on to these variations which use different fingerings. Work through these before moving on to a new key.

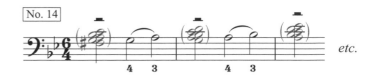

Drills: D Major

Arm Weight Exercises

a) Rest one arm on top of your other arm.
b) Experiment with making the top arm heavy, then light. Do this by letting the arm relax down with its own weight, not by pushing.

c) Rest your third finger on the surface of the key. Play each note by gently "releasing" your arm weight into the key as you did in step b). Your wrist should not move below the level of the key.

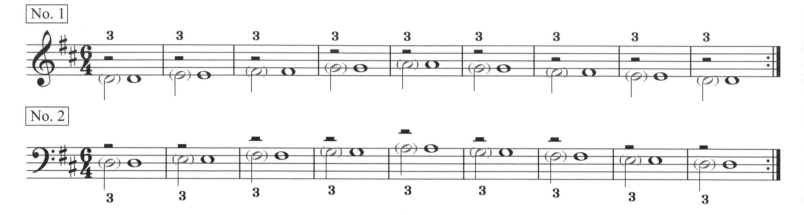

One-Note Drawbridge Exercises

a) Lift your arm about 6 inches above the key without bending at the wrist – as if it were a drawbridge. Flex your third finger so it feels strong.

b) Play each note by dropping your third finger into the key, releasing your arm weight with energy. Your wrist should not drop below key level.

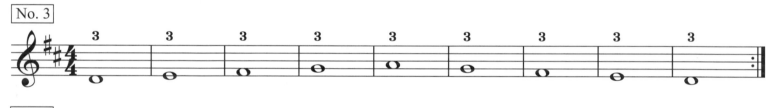

Open-Fifth Drawbridge Exercises

a) Lift your arm about 8 inches above the key without bending at the wrist – as if it were a drawbridge. Flex your thumb and fifth fingers so they feel strong.
b) Play each fifth by dropping your fingers into the keys,

releasing your arm weight with energy. Your wrist should not drop below key level.

c) Repeat steps a) & b), but this time lift your arm about 4 inches above the keys.

d) Repeat steps a) & b) lifting only 1 inch above the keys.

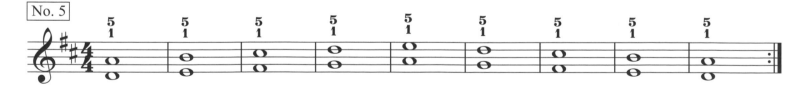

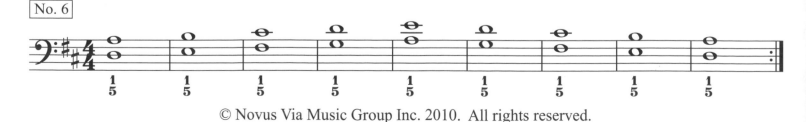

Beginning Rotation Exercises – Inward

a) Place your hand on the keys, fingers covering the five notes of the pentascale, with a good hand position.

b) Pretend you are getting ready to open a door. Rotate your hand inward, towards your thumb. The rotation motion should play the first note.

Observe that:
  i)   Your thumb will turn to be resting slightly on its nail.
  ii) Your elbow will move slightly away from your body.
  iii) The other fingers will raise above the keys.

c) Play the second note by rotating the other direction, back into position.

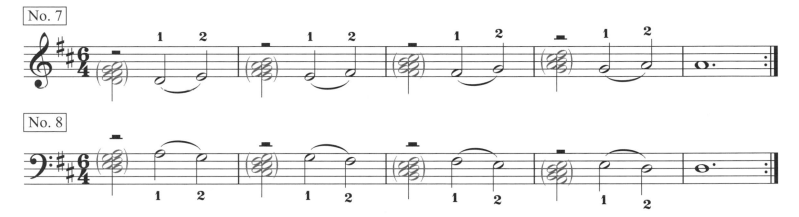

Beginning Rotation Exercises – Outward

a) Place your hand on the keys, fingers covering the five notes of the pentascale, with a good hand position.

b) Pretend you are getting ready to open a door. Rotate your hand outward, towards your 5th finger. The rotation motion should play the first note.

Observe that:
  i)   Your third finger will turn slightly onto its nail.
  ii) Your elbow will move slightly in to your body.
  iii) The thumb and second fingers will raise off the keys.

c) Play the second note by rotating the other direction, back into position.

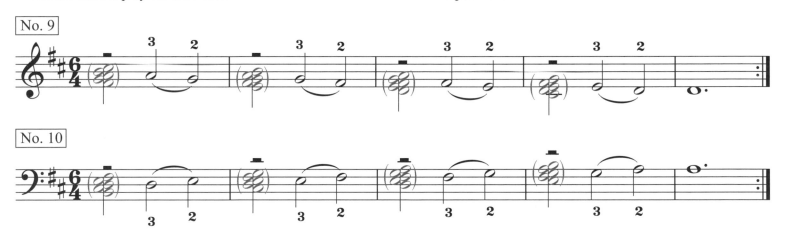

Fingering Variations

When you are able to play Drill nos. 7-10 with a fluid, even motion, move on to these variations which use different fingerings. Work through these before moving on to a new key.

Drills: A Major

Arm Weight Exercises

a) Rest one arm on top of your other arm.
b) Experiment with making the top arm heavy, then light. Do this by letting the arm relax down with its own weight, not by pushing.

c) Rest your third finger on the surface of the key. Play each note by gently "releasing" your arm weight into the key as you did in step b). Your wrist should not move below the level of the key.

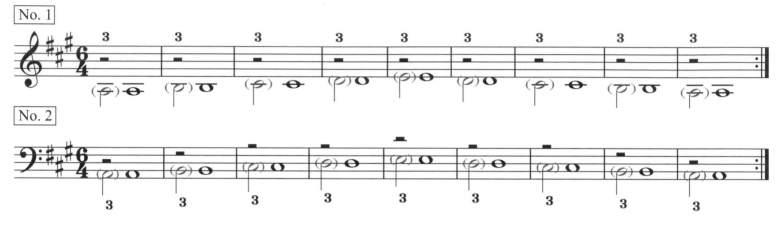

One-Note Drawbridge Exercises

a) Lift your arm about 6 inches above the key without bending at the wrist – as if it were a drawbridge. Flex your third finger so it feels strong.

b) Play each note by dropping your third finger into the key, releasing your arm weight with energy. Your wrist should not drop below key level.

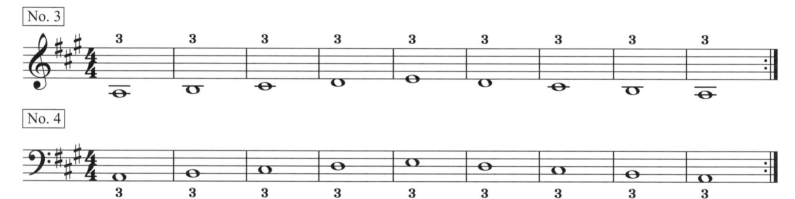

Open-Fifth Drawbridge Exercises

a) Lift your arm about 8 inches above the key without bending at the wrist – as if it were a drawbridge. Flex your thumb and fifth fingers so they feel strong.

b) Play each fifth by dropping your fingers into the keys,

releasing your arm weight with energy. Your wrist should not drop below key level.

c) Repeat steps a) & b), but this time lift your arm about 4 inches above the keys.

d) Repeat steps a) & b) lifting only 1 inch above the keys.

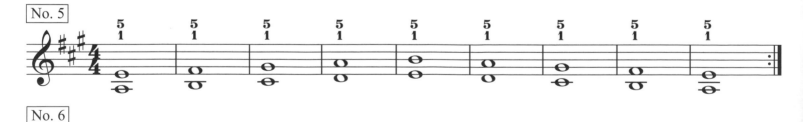

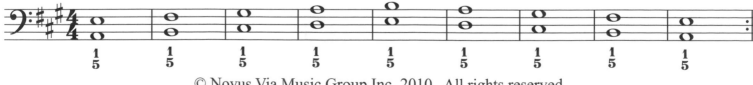

Beginning Rotation Exercises – Inward

a) Place your hand on the keys, fingers covering the five notes of the pentascale, with a good hand position.

b) Pretend you are getting ready to open a door. Rotate your hand inward, towards your thumb. The rotation motion should play the first note.

Observe that:

   i)   Your thumb will turn to be resting slightly on its nail.

   ii) Your elbow will move slightly away from your body.

   iii) The other fingers will raise above the keys.

c) Play the second note by rotating the other direction, back into position.

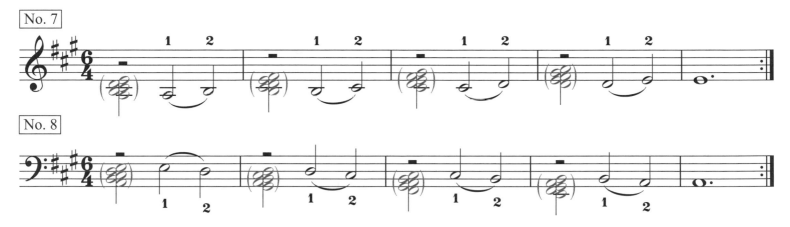

Beginning Rotation Exercises – Outward

a) Place your hand on the keys, fingers covering the five notes of the pentascale, with a good hand position.

b) Pretend you are getting ready to open a door. Rotate your hand outward, towards your 5th finger. The rotation motion should play the first note.

Observe that:

   i)   Your third finger will turn slightly onto its nail.

   ii) Your elbow will move slightly in to your body.

   iii) The thumb and second fingers will raise off the keys.

c) Play the second note by rotating the other direction, back into position.

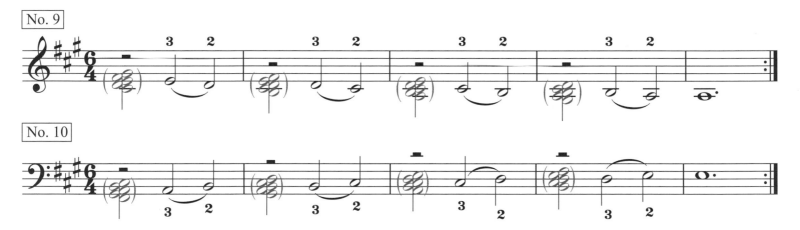

Fingering Variations

When you are able to play Drill nos. 7-10 with a fluid, even motion, move on to these variations which use different fingerings. Work through these before moving on to a new key.

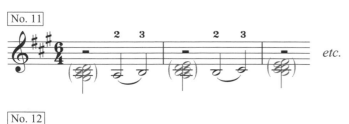

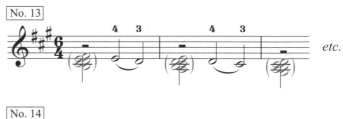

Drills: d harmonic minor

Arm Weight Exercises

a) Rest one arm on top of your other arm.
b) Experiment with making the top arm heavy, then light. Do this by letting the arm relax down with its own weight, not by pushing.

c) Rest your third finger on the surface of the key. Play each note by gently "releasing" your arm weight into the key as you did in step b). Your wrist should not move below the level of the key.

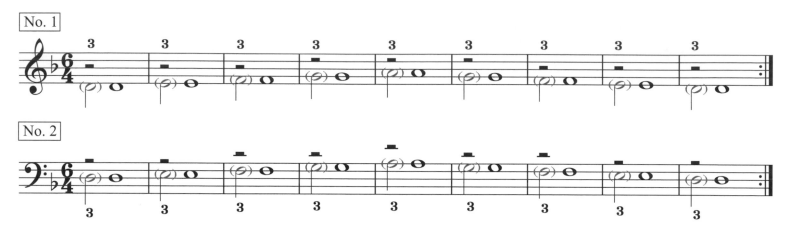

One-Note Drawbridge Exercises

a) Lift your arm about 6 inches above the key without bending at the wrist – as if it were a drawbridge. Flex your third finger so it feels strong.

b) Play each note by dropping your third finger into the key, releasing your arm weight with energy. Your wrist should not drop below key level.

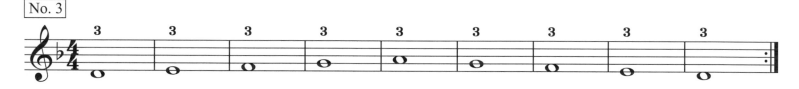

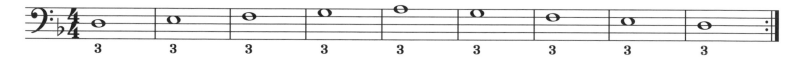

Open-Fifth Drawbridge Exercises

a) Lift your arm about 8 inches above the key without bending at the wrist – as if it were a drawbridge. Flex your thumb and fifth fingers so they feel strong.

b) Play each fifth by dropping your fingers into the keys,

releasing your arm weight with energy. Your wrist should not drop below key level.

c) Repeat steps a) & b), but this time lift your arm about 4 inches above the keys.

d) Repeat steps a) & b) lifting only 1 inch above the keys.

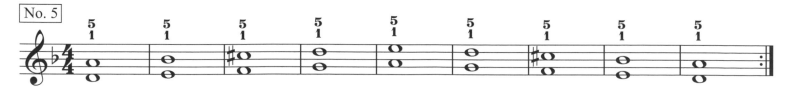

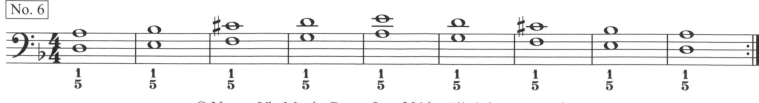

Beginning Rotation Exercises – Inward

a) Place your hand on the keys, fingers covering the five notes of the pentascale, with a good hand position.

b) Pretend you are getting ready to open a door. Rotate your hand inward, towards your thumb. The rotation motion should play the first note.

Observe that:
  i) Your thumb will turn to be resting slightly on its nail.
  ii) Your elbow will move slightly away from your body.
  iii) The other fingers will raise above the keys.

c) Play the second note by rotating the other direction, back into position.

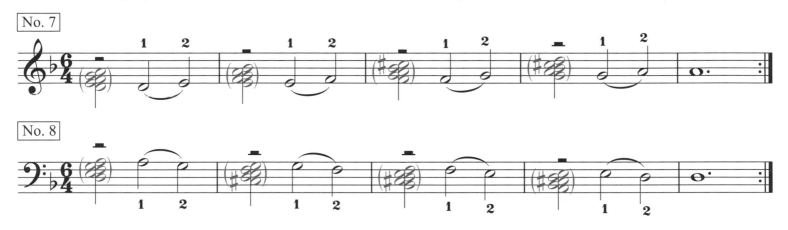

Beginning Rotation Exercises – Outward

a) Place your hand on the keys, fingers covering the five notes of the pentascale, with a good hand position.

b) Pretend you are getting ready to open a door. Rotate your hand outward, towards your 5th finger. The rotation motion should play the first note.

Observe that:
  i) Your third finger will turn slightly onto its nail.
  ii) Your elbow will move slightly in to your body.
  iii) The thumb and second fingers will raise off the keys.

c) Play the second note by rotating the other direction, back into position.

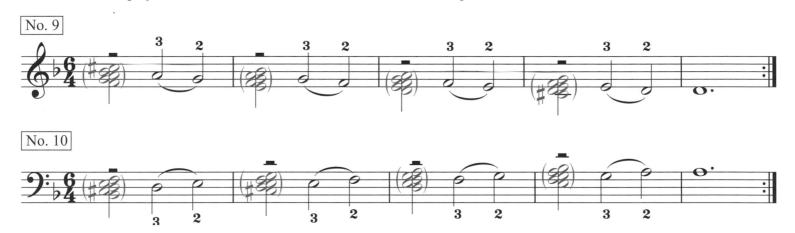

Fingering Variations

When you are able to play Drill nos. 7-10 with a fluid, even motion, move on to these variations which use different fingerings. Work through these before moving on to a new key.

Drills: a harmonic minor

Arm Weight Exercises

a) Rest one arm on top of your other arm.
b) Experiment with making the top arm heavy, then light. Do this by letting the arm relax down with its own weight, not by pushing.

c) Rest your third finger on the surface of the key. Play each note by gently "releasing" your arm weight into the key as you did in step b). Your wrist should not move below the level of the key.

One-Note Drawbridge Exercises

a) Lift your arm about 6 inches above the key without bending at the wrist – as if it were a drawbridge. Flex your third finger so it feels strong.

b) Play each note by dropping your third finger into the key, releasing your arm weight with energy. Your wrist should not drop below key level.

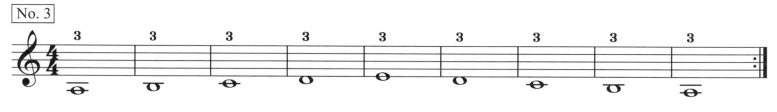

Open-Fifth Drawbridge Exercises

a) Lift your arm about 8 inches above the key without bending at the wrist – as if it were a drawbridge. Flex your thumb and fifth fingers so they feel strong.
b) Play each fifth by dropping your fingers into the keys,

releasing your arm weight with energy. Your wrist should not drop below key level.

c) Repeat steps a) & b), but this time lift your arm about 4 inches above the keys.
d) Repeat steps a) & b) lifting only 1 inch above the keys.

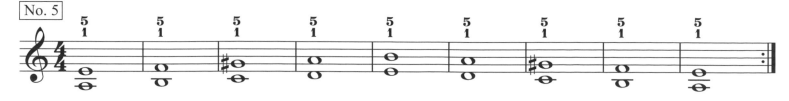

Beginning Rotation Exercises – Inward

a) Place your hand on the keys, fingers covering the five notes of the pentascale, with a good hand position.

b) Pretend you are getting ready to open a door. Rotate your hand inward, towards your thumb. The rotation motion should play the first note.

Observe that:

   i)   Your thumb will turn to be resting slightly on its nail.

   ii) Your elbow will move slightly away from your body.

   iii) The other fingers will raise above the keys.

c) Play the second note by rotating the other direction, back into position.

Beginning Rotation Exercises – Outward

a) Place your hand on the keys, fingers covering the five notes of the pentascale, with a good hand position.

b) Pretend you are getting ready to open a door. Rotate your hand outward, towards your 5th finger. The rotation motion should play the first note.

Observe that:

   i)   Your third finger will turn slightly onto its nail.

   ii) Your elbow will move slightly in to your body.

   iii) The thumb and second fingers will raise off the keys.

c) Play the second note by rotating the other direction, back into position.

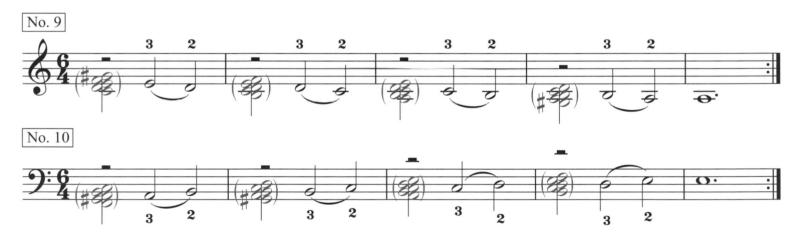

Fingering Variations

When you are able to play Drill nos. 7-10 with a fluid, even motion, move on to these variations which use different fingerings. Work through these before moving on to a new key.

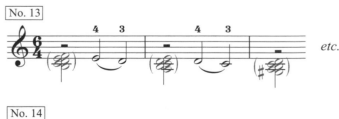

How to Use This Book

Many people consider Franz Liszt to be the greatest pianist who ever lived. He was a great believer in practicing technic. In his early years, he asked his students to spend two hours a day – on scales alone! This didn't include time spent on exercises, studies, or drills.

Most good pianists agree with Liszt; if you want to be good, you'll have to spend time practicing technic. In today's busy world, two hours a day on scales is too much for many students. But the more time you spend working on your technic, in every way, the better your playing will be.

Not sure how to proceed? The *American Popular Piano Technic* books are here to help!

The Learning Ladder

Initial Thoughts

Daily practice is essential. If you don't have a lot of time, work on your technic a little bit – but don't skip it!

■ Many teachers think you should do technical work for about 1/4 to 1/3 of your total practice time. It doesn't have to be done all at once. Some pianists like to work on technic at the beginning of a practice session, in order to warm up their fingers and their brain. Others prefer to do it later in the day, or to do several mini-sessions throughout the day. Experiment and see what works for you.

■ In general, it's better to repeat a smaller number of exercises many times, than to do lots of exercises a few times. Best, of course, is to do lots of exercises lots of times!

First Steps

Students often begin practicing the patterns hands separately. Play hands together when your teacher says you are ready.

■ Pick a key.
   1. Silently sing the exercise to yourself. Every detail of pitch, counting, and dynamics should be exact. Don't play until everything is clear in your mind.
   2. Play at a steady tempo without stopping. Aim for a tempo that is slow enough that everything is perfect.

■ Add a new key every few weeks, but don't forget to allow time for review of old keys.

■ Visit our website for other great ideas to vary your technical practice.

Checking

Technic is a visual, experiential and above all, a listening process.

■ Look.
   It's a good idea to memorize the basic technical patterns so you can look at your hands. (When sightreading and learning repertoire, it's a good idea **not** to look at your hands, but technical work is different).
   1. Make sure your hand position is good.

   2. Fingers should be in appropriate position, as directed. When not in preparation or use, they should be relaxed and close to the keys.
   3. Make sure hands mirror each other when completing the same movement. Hand position, degree of rotation, and finger placement should look the same in each hand.

■ Feel.
   It can be difficult, sometimes, to feel the difference between tension, which is bad, and flexion, which is necessary. A flexed finger feels strong – not stiff or claw-like. You should feel your finger relax after the note has been sounded. When you flex your fingers, check your shoulder, elbow, and wrist to make sure they are not clenched.

■ Listen.
   Good piano tone sounds rich, full, and resonant. Listen closely to make sure accented notes are strong, not "bangy".

Some Basic Tips

Audiate

Audiation is the ability to hear music in your mind without the presence of sound. It's a skill that all good musicians must possess. So "audiate" before you play. Don't start playing without singing silently to yourself. Then, play and try to match the sound you created in your brain.

Slow Practice

The surest path to brilliant, fast technic is controlled, repetitive practice at a deliberate, slow tempo. Spend a significant portion of your time practicing slowly. Listen carefully and check carefully.

■ Is every note rhythmically exact? All quarter notes should be precisely the same length. Whole notes should be exactly four times as long as quarter notes. Are yours?

■ Does every note have a full, rounded tone quality?

■ Are all the notes tonally even? You shouldn't hear some notes lighter or more full than others. Liszt told his students that nothing should ever be abrupt or uneven. Pay special attention to your thumb!

■ Are you playing at the correct dynamic? Are all notes dynamically matched? No notes should sound "thumping" or, conversely, too soft in relation to the others.

Repetition

There are many opinions about the optimal number of times to practice. For us, the magic number is "5". 5 times is the basic number of repetitions, do 10 times for a good workout, and play 15 times for the greatest effectiveness. An important factor in improving fundamentals is: **work on them—and do it often!!**

The root word for technic is the ancient Greek tekhnikos – "about art". So practice these excerpts with full artistry and with love. Let the fact that they are musically simple help you focus your full attention on the technical challenges. Repeat often, concentrate — and listen closely! Your diligence will be rewarded.